Migratory Words

Migratory Words

Moumin Quazi

LITERARY PRESS
LAMAR UNIVERSITY

ISBN: 978-1-942956-33-4
Library of Congress Control Number: 2016951397

Manufactured in The United States of America
Front Cover: Saleem Photography, "Parvaaz"

Lamar University Literary Press
Beaumont, Texas

Acknowledgments

I am grateful to the editors of the following publications for publishing some of the writing in this volume.

Amarillo Bay, August 2016
CCTE Studies Volume LXX
Concho River Review
Elvis: Back in the Stacks
Is This Forever, Or What? Poems and Paintings from Texas
Prentice Hall 8th Grade Literature Textbook (Volume 1)
Red River Review 55 and 58
South Asian Review XXVI, XXVII, and XXIX
Tom
Voices de la Luna: A Quarterly Poetry and Arts Magazine 7.5
Voices: San Antonio College Multiculturalism Journal
Writing Texas, 2013-2014, 2014-2015, and *2015-2016*

Thank you, Abba and Mom, for originally publishing me in San Francisco back in 1962.

Thank you, Rahim and David, and Sherry, Micah, Carl, Pam, Masood, Suzanne, Marinell, Rifat, Jessica, Ben, Lennon, Kai, Brenda, Hannah, Ben, and my other relatives too numerous to mention, for joining me along the way.

Thank you to friends who have stayed constant throughout the years: Troy and Vanessa, Carla, Blake, Marguerite, Donell, Nancy, Dian, Glen, Bill, Gail, Dan, Alan, Ani, Robin, and also Mary and Dierk, and Anne and Bob.

Thanks to Charlie (from my TCU days), Andy Stanley (we never just called him "Andy"), Dayne, and Aaron (from my Dallas days), Scott, Melissa, and Winda (from my Denton days), Neeta, Corinna, and Juanita (from my San Antonio days), Arch and Edy Lou (from my Plainview days), Daniella and Diann (from my Lamar days), and (in Stephenville) Dell, Shay, James, Jeri, my Tarleton colleagues, and the many others that I just can't list here, for space sake.

I offer a very special thanks to Naomi Shihab Nye, for publishing "Migrant Words" in a book, Jerry Bradley, for publishing my first poem in a journal, and Jerry Craven, for publishing my first book.

I thank also Don and Dolores Vann for believing in me like no others ever have. My admiration for you is almost as boundless as my affection.

Thanks to Marilyn Robitaille, the colleague who helps make my life the most interesting party ever.

Thanks to The Beatles, Arthur Conan Doyle, Charles Dickens, Robert Browning, Salman Rushdie, Jerry Lewis, Carol Burnett, Dick Van Dyke, Tim Conway, Gene Wilder, Margaret Atwood, Radiohead, Pat Metheny, Peter Gabriel, Jerry Seinfeld, and The Marx Brothers. With you, I know I'll never walk alone.

A special thanks to those who have passed away (sometimes more than once). Margot, I love you, though I know my affection for cats, and my solitary habits must haunt you terribly.

Thanks to PJ, the best teammate I've ever had. You are my wellspring of comfort and delight.

In a nutshell, thanks to those who nurtured, challenged, loved, and hurt me along the way. Without you, I wouldn't have become a writer.

And, finally, thanks to all the animals who opened my heart to love deeper (that goes for you who are reading this book).

Recent books from Lamar University Literary Press

Bobby Aldridge, *An Affair of the Stilled Heart*
Michael Baldwin, *Lone Star Heart*
Robert Bonazzi, *Awakened by Surprise*
Jerry Bradley, and Ulf Kirchdorfer(eds), *The Great American
        Wise Ass Poetry Anthology*
David Bowles, *Flower, Song, Dance: Aztec and Mayan Poetry*
Jerry Bradley, *Crownfeathers and Effigies*
Christopher Carmona, Rob Johnson, and Chuck Taylor, *The
        Beatest State in the Union*
Stan Crawford, *Resisting Gravity*
Glover Davis, *My Cap of Darkness*
Larry Griffin *Cedar Plums*
Robert M. Davis, *Levels of Incompetence: An Academic Life*
Gerald Duff, *Memphis Mojo*
Ted L. Estess, *Fishing Spirit Lake*
Katherine Hoerth, *Goddess Wears Cowboy Boots*
Lynn Hoggard, *Motherland, Stories and Poems from Louisiana*
Gretchen Johnson, *The Joy of Deception*
Tom Mack and Andrew Geyer (eds), *A Shared Voice*
Janet McCann, *The Crone at the Casino*
Harold Raley, *Louisiana Rogue*
Carol Coffee Reposa, *Underground Musicians*
Jim Sanderson, *Trashy Behavior*
Jim Sanderson, *Sanderson's Fiction Writing Manual*
Jan Seale, *Appearances*
Jan Seale, *The Parkinson Poems*
Melvin Sterne, *The Number You Have Reached*
Steven Schroeder, *the moon, not the finger, pointing*
Steven Schroeder, *What's Love Got to do With It?*
Robert Wexelblatt, *The Artist Wears Rough Clothing*
Jonas Zdanys and Steven Schroeder, *Red Stones*

For information on these and other
Lamar University Literary Press books, go to
www.lamar.edu/literarypress

CONTENTS

Fictions

Poems

Nonfictions

Fictions

Three Favorite Words

We were three men sitting around a table, a father and his two sons, alone together because we had just lost a loved one. She had passed suddenly from cancer. And for those who don't believe that people can be here today and then gone only 24 days after a diagnosis, it's true. It really does happen. What started as a seemingly normal case of anemia turned out to be ovarian cancer gone into her colon and then lymphatic system. And, just like that, a husband of 37 years and two stepsons who felt like her "real" children were punching through a fog of surprise and grief unlike anything they had known before.

Outside it was strangely cold. A frozen fog had settled in, leaving crystals of ice on every blade of grass, barren branch, and unfortunate flower. It was beautiful in a strange way, almost lunar but with moisture. Inside the quiet house, the father and his sons were going over the details of the next day when she would be buried. She would be ceremonially washed by two women from the Islamic center, and then wrapped in a simple sheet. We would be invited into the room where her body was, a place that would turn out to be more like an empty fish market after it had been hosed down for the night. Her body would be covered except for her face, though after a few of us had said goodbye, the two women would wrap the cloth around her face, too. And then we would pick her up and put her into a simple pine box, making sure to position her body so that it would be leaning toward Mecca when she was laid in the ground with her head facing eastward.

The two sons listened to their father as he went over the other details of the coming day, letting them know that since German law forbid being buried in only a sheet, he had to purchase a coffin, but that we were going to place in it several handfuls of dirt from the front and back gardens that she had toiled in for so many years. We remembered together how much pleasure and work maintaining a yard was in Bavaria. While we were sitting there, one of the sons said that tomorrow we would hopefully experience a phenomenon that was captured by his favorite word. We asked him what that word was, and he answered, "apricity," that experience of the warmth of sunshine on your face on a winter's day.

"That's a great word. You don't hear it anymore."

"Truly." A silence followed that indicated submersion into thought.

"And what's your favorite word, Abba?"

"Aurora borealis."

"Mmmmm. That's a good one! We'll count it, even though it's really two words."

"Yes, but they are my favorite words in English."

"Have you ever seen the Northern Lights in your travels?" we asked him.

"Yes, in Alaska."

"Mmmmm. How neat."

Finally, he asked the eldest son, "What is your favorite word? It's your turn now."

He answered, "Callipygian."

"Callipygian?"

"Yes, it means, 'having beautiful buttocks' as in, 'that statue of Aphrodite has divinely callipygian assets.'"

For a few moments, the three men sat around the table and chuckled that the Greeks had given that quality a word of its own.

Each of the favorite words came from Latin or Greek. Apricity came from "*apericus*," which is where "apricot" derived, a fruit that even looks like a miniature sun. "Aurora" came from the Roman goddess of dawn (another sun phenomenon) and "borealis" came from the Greek "north wind." "Callipygian" just came from the word for "beautiful" ("*kallos*") and "behind" ("*puge*") in Greek.

Just for a moment, pain was subsumed by wordplay and riddles.

The next morning, all that went away until the three of them were standing at the now-covered graveside. The dirt had been patted down, leaving a mound that everyone knows somehow. The wet cold stabbed through the layers of clothing and overcoats. There was no sunshine peeking through the clouds that day.

Later, when the three men were at home, it was very quiet. The younger son had gone up the stairs, leaving the eldest son alone with their Abba, who turned and said, "Do you think 'callipygian' can refer to men, as well as women?" His lips curled up just ever so slightly, recalling the last night's brief respite from grief.

"I'm sure it does, Abba."

"Well then, your brother is in good shape. He has callipygian qualities. As for you, I want you to work on losing some weight."

Now, he was channeling his dearly departed wife, who would have asked the same.

"You're right. I definitely need to do that. It's certainly what she would have wanted, too."

"Yes, it most certainly is." He said this quietly and looked down where he was now seated. "I need to tell you something."

"Of course, Abba," the son said, reaching out and holding his father's hand.

"I just wanted to let you know that I never really saw the aurora borealis."

"Oh...that's okay, Abba. I just thought you might have, during your travels."

"Well, yes. I might have, but I really didn't, though I do think they are beautiful. I felt bad that I misled you because I actually never did see them, and I exaggerated a little."

"It's okay, Abba." In the silence, the eldest son held his father's hand. "I appreciate that you told me. It was difficult last night, I know. It's okay, Abba."

The new widower closed his eyes and tilted his head upward, and in that moment took in the apricity from his son's love.

Gone Bananas

Maybe it was because of his intense longing to be with others that Charlie first began to have an inordinate craving for bananas. Perhaps he was drawn to the clustered nature of that strange but wondrous fruit. Or maybe he identified with the solitude that comes with being torn away from the others and being suddenly alone and more easily bruised.

Charlie was newly divorced. Well, not exactly newly—it had been two years, but he had found it hard to re-enter the dating scene. He was thirty-nine years old, and though he was constantly around lots of lovely people at the school where he taught, he still went home to an empty apartment. Well, not exactly empty—it had three cats in it that Charlie got to keep after the divorce. Simon, Sidney, and Sophie. Other than felines, the apartment was a far cry from the troubles and joys of married life, with the bickering and the laughter and the barks of dogs and the subtle comfort that comes from the mere presence of another human, even if that human doesn't always get along with you.

Whatever the reason, one day, just a few months before his 40th birthday, Charlie found that he constantly wanted to eat bananas. He couldn't stop. As soon as he awoke in the morning, he wanted a banana. When he went to lunch, it had to be a banana. Snack, dinner, snack. Banana, banana, banana.

His friends were the first to notice Charlie's sudden thing for bananas, and were the first to offer a variety of explanations for his new food-of-choice.

Tom, who wore button-down shirts and khakis, and was slightly bald, offered a Scientific explanation: "You must have a potassium deficiency. Do you find yourself cramping during times of exertion? Maybe you're hypoglycemic. Have you considered going to the doctor for some blood work?"

Trish, who wore hemp skirts, tee-shirts with no bra, and had frizzed her beautifully straight hair, offered a Naturalistic explanation: "You probably have a desire to go back to the jungle to get back in touch with your bestial nature. Do you find yourself wanting to lounge around naked or play on swingsets? Have you considered Primal Scream therapy?"

Cal, who wore white turtlenecks, trendy glasses, and had spiky hair, offered a Freudian explanation: "You must have some latent homosexuality that you're not dealing with. You like bananas, huh? That's the ultimate fruit-phallus, you know! What you need is to get laid. Have you considered going out with my cousin? He's really nice."

Tim, who always only wore black, offered a Color Symbologist explanation: "You must be subconsciously confronting your fears. Bananas are yellow and yellow symbolizes cowardice. You are somehow devouring your fear of fear. Have you considered going to group therapy?"

Winda, who always wore a tennis outfit, offered a Jungian explanation: "You must be longing to go back to your childhood and the good memories associated with your youth. Your inner-child desires the crushed bananas of your infancy, the banana splits of your pre-adolescence, and all the times you got sick and were nursed back to health with those floating bananas in the clear, red jello of your innocence. Also, maybe bananas are like little Christmas gifts you get to unwrap one-by-one. Have you considered visiting your hometown? And don't forget to call your mother."

And finally, Dave, who wore jeans and pullover sweaters and a What Would Jesus Do? bracelet, offered a Theological explanation: "You must be feeling guilty about your past. Perhaps the Holy Spirit is trying to get you to leave your sin. You know the forbidden fruit wasn't really an apple—it was a banana! Why do you think Eve was so attracted to it? The Tree of the Knowledge of Good and Evil was a banana tree! Have you considered accepting Jesus into your heart as your personal lord and savior?"

Bananas.

One morning soon thereafter, Charlie woke up and decided to see a psychiatrist to find out what *she* thought was wrong with him. After he had filled out six sheets of a lengthy questionnaire, Dr. Marie McQueen whose long, dark hair and olive skin only slightly distracted him, asked him about his problem. He said, "I can't seem to get enough bananas. Morning, Noon, and Night, I want to eat bananas."

She looked at him, rifled through the papers on her

desk, and seemed to think for a short while. She looked at him again, and finally she said, "Have you tried the Central Market on the corner of Main and Miranda? They're always stocked up on them."

Charlie fell in love with Marie, and they ended up marrying and moving to Costa Rica, where they bought a banana plantation together. Nowadays, "Mare" practices holistic therapy, and Charlie supervises the picking of bananas all day, eating as many as he wants throughout the morning and afternoon, until he can come home to his wife.

Oh, and every now and then, he eats a nice piece of baked fish.

Tire Swing

The day is warm, and the little neighborhood where Charlie lives is just waking up. Mrs. Garrett is brewing coffee. Her cotton nightgown is tied tightly around her frail body, though no one is there to see them if one of her body parts were to be exposed. Her Folgers is percolating in an old G.E. coffee maker, blurping an aroma that always reminds her of life when the kids lived at home and her husband George was alive. But that was a long time ago. She is looking out the window and spies two redbirds chasing each other from tree to tree, their high chirps piercing the air. Across the street, Jack Rogers is watching the morning television news show, not because he cares what's going on in the world, but because he has a crush on the morning anchorwoman, Paula Sandler. Jack Roger's wife, Teresa, suspects his infatuation, but plays along with it, egging him on from the bathroom with, "What's Sandles got to say this morning?" Jack Rogers mutters, "Nothin'," and then adjusts himself on his recliner and watches his show. Across the street from Jack Rogers and Teresa, a dog owner named Ken walks Skimpy, the dachshund born without a tail. Skimpy is a silver-dapple mix and darts in and out of bushes, sporadically straining the leash that Ken delights to hold. Jack Rogers calls the dog without a tail

"Stubby," and wonders how in the hell Ken can bend down every morning and pick up "Stubby shit," even if Ken's hand is in a plastic bag. Clearly, Jack Rogers has never owned an animal.

In the meantime, Charlie is taking a pair of his favorite jeans and cutting the legs off just above the knees. He is forty-two years old and he can't remember the last time he wore cut-offs. He fishes an old tee-shirt out of his dresser drawer and slips it on. It's a little snug on his six-foot frame, and it flairs out just a little around his middle, though no one would ever consider him out-of-shape. He puts on his cut-offs, and realizes how white his feet and toes are. His legs are much whiter than his otherwise brown skin is, and his lanky legs look especially long in his retro outfit. Charlie seems satisfied and goes out to his backyard and picks up a tire he got from a local service station the day before. He rolls the tire into the front yard, leans it up against a tree, and goes to the trunk of his car and pulls out a length of rope. He goes back to the tree, knots one end of the rope, and throws it over the biggest branch. He ties it off and ties the tire to the other end of rope, creating a swing. The rope is thick and the sisal burns Charlie's hands when he pulls the rope to tighten the knots. But he is ready now.

Ken is going back into his house now, but Skimpy really wants to check out the new swing next door. His rump is moving furiously back and forth, but Ken pulls the leash gently and Skimpy walks into the house, while looking back over his shoulder. The door slams shut, and from the bedroom, Ken's girlfriend, Michelle, asks how the walk went. Ken says, "Fine. Skimpy did his business and the guy across the street made a tire swing." Michelle thinks to herself, "That's kinda strange," and rolls over. Skimpy jumps up into the bed and burrows under the sheets, beside Michelle. She snuggles and snoozes, while Ken throws away the plastic bag and washes his hands. He will leave for work soon, too, leaving the "wife and kid" to sleep as long as they want. Next door, Teresa is ready for work now, too, and has just kissed Jack Rogers on the cheek before picking up her briefcase and driving off in her white Rav-4. She sees Charlie as she drives past, and thinks to herself that she's never even noticed that tree before, much less the tire-swing and that older man in his shorts. Mrs. Garrett is now pouring her coffee into a mug with a painting of the Grand Canyon on it, that her oldest son's family gave her from their last family vacation. Mrs. Garrett stirs in a little Splenda and moves to the table, but not before first noticing that that young man across the way is rocking back and forth in his new tire swing. Oh, that brings back a memory of when she was seven and went to the park with her papa and how he pushed her higher and higher into the air until she thought she was going to go all the way around. She catches her breath and sits down and sips from her mug.

Now that Jack Rogers has the house and bathroom to himself, he finishes his morning routine, shaving, and brushing his teeth. He's a huge guy (so big that he always goes by two names), with broad shoulders and big, thick arms and hands. He's only forty nine, but people swear he's really in his early sixties. Some people just look older than they are, he says to them when they act amazed. Whiles he's brushing, he notices out of the corner of his eye that something is moving outside his bathroom window. He looks out and sees his neighbor swinging in the tire, every now and then kicking the tree to keep him moving. Jack Rogers mutters under his breath, "What the grunt is that guy doing?"

Charlie swings all day long in the shade of his front yard tree, only occasionally taking a break to go inside and have a bite or get a can of soda. Teresa drives home. Ken and Michelle go about their business and walk Skimpy that evening. Not long after, they will eat some pasta with chicken and a salad. Skimpy will hope that a little bit of something falls to the floor. It will. Jack Rogers and Teresa eat their dinner, an order of take-out barbeque that Teresa picked up on the way home. Mrs. Garrett opens a can of soup for her dinner, and watches "Wheel of Fortune" as she eats. Charlie goes inside finally, takes a shower, and has a bowl of SpaghettiO's with meatballs, followed by a bowl of Fruit Loops for dessert. He is surprisingly tired, he thinks and falls asleep on the couch as the television flickers its prime time and then late night shows, unwatched.

For nearly three months, Charlie occupies his days in his cut-offs and t-shirt, one day playing catch with an old ball and glove. One day hiking around, exploring. He sits in his yard, looking at doodle bugs and other tiny creatures that usually go unnoticed. He goes under the house and maps in his mind where the rooms of his home are, where the pipes lead, where the drains drain to. He finds an old Indian-head penny in a crack between the floorboards. He will put this in his treasure box later.

Other days, he puts on some roller skates, kicks a soccer ball for hours, plays hacky sack, and flies a diamond-shaped kite made with newspaper and sticks. He uses old dryer sheets stapled to a thin strip of old sheet for the tail. The kite gets off the ground for a while but then gets stuck in his tree after a gust catches him off guard. Other days, Charlie even knocks on people's doors, to ask if they can come out to play.

Day after day, even in the rain, he goes outside, and plays.

The neighborhood can't resist speculating. Teresa wonders, "Has he had a nervous breakdown?" "Is he playing a joke on the neighborhood?" wonders Ken. "Doesn't he have a job?" thinks Michelle. Mrs. Garret brushes aside the thought, "Is that young man a pervert?" and then feels guilty for even thinking it. She bakes Charlie a batch of Toll House cookies with walnuts, which he gratefully accepts and eats later with a tall glass of cold milk. "Do you think he might be a millionaire?" Michelle asks Ken. "I betcha he's retarded" Jack Rogers says. And finally, Skimpy the tailless dachshund and Charlie have by now become close buddies.

Near the end of the summer, the neighborhood has a block party, at Charlie's invitation. Even Jack Rogers finds that he is kind of excited to mingle with his neighbors, who by now have found a common focal point of curiosity in Charlie. And so it goes, that on a hot Saturday in late August, everyone comes out to play.

Finally, as summer winds down, and the promise of autumn whispers from beyond the branches, Charlie ties tire swings to everyone's trees. And then, he goes inside, and readies himself for the days ahead.

Now, Charlie is at his desk, writing a story about Mrs. Garrett, Jack Rogers and Teresa, Ken and Michelle and Skimpy, since he had always wondered what it would be like, as a college professor, to live a life as fun and free of care as everyone *thought* he lived.

The next day he goes back to his university, a lot more tanned, a lot more refreshed, and a lot saner, with a short story in his folder, that he hopes one day will be included in a book.

Under the Robes

"Have you ever noticed that the way Christ is often depicted, with outstretched arms nailed to the cross, that those arms look like the fallopian tubes on one of those medical diagrams in the examination room at a doctor's office?" Martin said before he bit into his burrito. Juice dripped down his chin before he dabbed it with his carefully folded paper napkin.

"Jeez, you're blasphemous," said Kathy, strawberry blond hair looking radiant while the sun backlit her head in the booth of the fastfood taco joint.

"No, I don't mean it to be. I mean, from that perspective, then, his body is the womb out of which Christians are 'born again.'" Martin seemed happy with his theological assessment, then let out a muffled burp into his cupped hand. "Excuse me."

Ever since she met him, she always enjoyed Martin's meanderings into the woods of philosophy and theology and whatever else hooked his mental energy at the time. His tallness, brown hair, smooth skin, and tootsie-roll eyes turned her on, too. They were both second year grad students, and had found in each other a welcome retreat from the pressures of having to fit in at school.

Martin continued his little-engine-that-could train of thought. "If there was anyone in touch with his anima, Jesus was that guy, don't you think?"

"What the hell is an 'anima'?" Kathy said as she cracked into her crispy beef taco.

"It's the Jungian idea of the female principle, the animal soul, the passive soul."

"As opposed to the male, rational, and active soul? Give me a break. That kind of binary opposition is so goofy. Sometimes, when you say stuff like that, I wanna bite into your dimpled cheek and just chew on it."

Martin blushed at the compliment folded into that beasty threat like the sour cream in the combo burrito he was nearly finished eating. "I'm just saying that it seems that Jesus was a guy deeply in touch with his feminine side." Kathy didn't mind that Martin wouldn't let go of this thought. He had recently converted to Christianity and was exploring the different aspects of the gospels he had only just started to read. He picked his words from memory: "In the Gospel of John, it says that near the cross, when the Romans were putting Jesus to death, his mother was nearby, and when he saw her from up there, he said to the disciple with her, 'Dear woman, here is your son,' and to the disciple, 'Here is your mother,' and from that time on, the disciple took her into his home."

"Last summer, I went to Mexico City and saw the Cathedral of the Virgin of Guadalupe." Kathy sipped her coke.

"Alone?"

Now it was her turn to blush at Martin's microflash

of jealousy. "I went with my mom and gramma, before she passed away."

"Oh, I'm sorry, Kate."

"It's okay. Gramma was in her eighties and she had always wanted to see that image of the Virgin, before she died. She wasn't even a Catholic; she just liked the romance of that story. I mean, Mary appeared to a no-name guy in the Mexican outback, and brought the message of Jesus to the unprivileged. I wanted to see what Juan Diego supposedly saw."

"So that's where you get your spirituality, huh?

"I guess. When I entered the Church of the Virgin, I felt compelled to get on my knees and shuffle to the front of the church and pray for my gramma. It was really hot outside, but the floor was cool to the touch. My knees almost immediately started to hurt, but I didn't care. Pilgrims and poseurs alike made their way to the front, where the image was framed and hanging on the wall. Beautiful trumpet music was blasting away, but I almost couldn't hear it. All I could think about was how all these other people were putting so much trust in their prayers to the Virgin Mary, and how sore my knees were, and was my head covered properly, and was my dress concealing my legs enough, and could the Virgin please give my gramma painless passage into heaven, and would I ever meet a nice guy like you." Martin reached over and lightly squeezed Kathy's hand. It was cold from the coke she had been holding. "Then, we all went to this place behind the altar where you can get a closer look at the image."

"What do you mean, image?"

"Well, supposedly, it's not a painting or a photograph. It's a supernatural image of a woman with her robe all starry and blue. It was supposed to be kind of painted on the robe that Juan Diego was wearing the second time she appeared to him. But, they've apparently never figured out where the image came from—like that shroud in Turin, I think." This was the kind of talk that made Martin love Kathy.

"That image—as in *imagine*—is an enigma. Like you," Martin said.

"Stop it. You're making fun of me now."

"No. I like it when you talk like this. Go on. What happened next?"

"I went behind the altar to see the image. There was a line of people waiting to stand in front of it and look up to see the Virgin."

"Did you look up her skirt?"

That urge to bite his face was coming back.

"They say you can see Juan Diego's body in the reflection of her eye. Isn't that cool?"

"Very."

"The funny thing was, that to make it where lots of people could look, they've put this conveyor belt, like the kind at airports, in front of it. Two of them. When I got to the place, I found myself in line to ride a conveyor belt that runs along below, in front of the elevated image. And just a few minutes earlier, I was on my knees, sweating it out."

"Old fashioned adoration mixed with a technological worship belt that whirred you in front of the Virgin for a closer look up her sacred robe."

"Marty, stop it! You're going to go to hell." She smiled and squirmed in her seat a little, checking around to see if anyone heard her crass boyfriend.

"Actually, this reminds me of my grandma. Let's go." They crumpled up their paper wrappings and took their trays to the trash bins, unloading them as they walked out of the restaurant. Martin opened the door, and Kathy walked out first. The air was hot, a stark contrast to the air-conditioned booth they had just left. Martin followed close behind as they made their way to his '72 Pinto station wagon, wood paneling and all.

***

Later that night, Kathy was getting ready for bed. Martin was already tucked in. He was a new Christian, but he wasn't a prude. Their love justified their spending the night together, so neither of them felt there was any moral dilemma. The sheets were cool. Cotton. High thread count. Very comfortable. Martin could hear Kathy humming to herself in the bathroom.

"Marty?"

"Yeah?"

"Earlier—you said—that my—trip to Mexico City—reminded you—of your grandmother." Kathy was now flossing her teeth, causing her to speak in spurts of language.

"Yeah. The Virgin's robe and Diego's image reminded me of the first time I saw an adult vagina." Martin looked toward to the bathroom. "I was eight."

"Oh, my God! What did you say?" She had stopped flossing.

"You made me remember the first time I saw an

31

older woman's, you know, pussy."

Kathy nearly swallowed her mouthwash but managed to spit it out before she hurried to the bed. "Come again?"

"I was playing hide'n'go seek with my younger brother, and I hid under my grandma's bed in her old 2-story Victorian house." They cuddled as he talked. Kathy didn't know whether to be excited to hear what was coming next or just horrified. "I was still and quiet and all alone—well hidden from everybody, especially my brother who was scurrying from room to room, looking for me, his unwittingly mischievous older brother."

"How old were you?"

"Eight." Martin turned off the bedside table lamp. Some secrets could only be told in the dark, he thought. "Apparently, I was so well hidden that my grandma didn't know I was under her bed when she walked to the side of it and began doing her weekly ironing."

"How old was *she*?"

"Does it matter? She was my *grandma*, for god's sake. Anyway, I don't know when it came into my little head to slide out enough to look under her white terrycloth robe, but it did, and I did."

"Like a goofy, little mechanic on an imaginary grease monkey, wheeling out from under the covers of the bed and under the cover of your grandma's white robe."

"I lay there still and breathless, staring up, up, and up those long, white legs until I saw a dark patch of hair—to me, an indiscriminate patch, not hiding anything in particular."

Now, the dark hid his embarrassment.

Martin said, "I didn't know what mysteries were hidden under that tuft, what secrets my grandma's pubes kept. All I did know was the rocking rhythm of my grandma's body swaying ever so gently as she pressed her iron to the clothes on her board." Kathy was reminding herself to breathe. "Every now and then, I could hear the hiss of steam as she sprinkled water onto the clothes and pressed the hot iron down onto the wet cloth." His heart beat hard in his chest, just like back then. "I watched her iron like that, my head hidden under her robe, eyes transfixed on her thighs and dark patch of adultness for only a few minutes, finally pulling myself back under the bed. I was soaking in my own sweat."

"Oh, my, god. I can't believe you saw your gramma's bush." At the sound of her giggly voice, Martin breathed out his relief.

"I waited until she was finished ironing when I finally squirmed out from under the bed. My grandma turned around and asked, 'Where have you been?' Playing hide and seek. Nobody caught me, so I came out to start a new game. 'Well, be careful, dear.' I will, grandma! Believe me!"

Martin felt Kathy's grip harden on his arm as she pulled him closer to herself. "I can't believe it."

"From that time on, I saw my grandma and her bathrobe in a different light."

"I guess so."

"She wasn't wearing any panties under that robe—aren't grandmas supposed to wear panties?"

Both Martin's and Kathy's eyes had, by now, adjusted to the dark. She looked at Martin, wondering what other secrets he had been able to keep. He said, "She had a black patch of hair between her legs! What a revelation!"

He caressed the curve of Kathy's back, every now and then stopping to pick on a rough spot of skin. "I had no idea that that hair concealed lips and more lips and a clitoris and a birth canal and so much more," he whispered.

"What do you mean, so much more?" she whispered back.

"My grandma had 'female problems,' and she passed away from bladder cancer less than a year later. She was fifty-four. I was nine." Martin thought for a second; Kathy was remembering her own gramma. He said, "Kate, sweetheart, at the time, I had no idea that I would be privy to a sight usually only reserved for a mother's, then a doctor's, then a husband's, and then finally, a mortician's gaze."

Martin put his right hand between Kathy's thighs and felt the warmth of her body as he held her closer with his left. He hadn't thought of it for years, but now the thought crept to him, as if peeking its head out from under a bed: was he to blame for his grandma's death? If he hadn't stolen a look at her forbidden body, would she have lived to meet his children some day? Or was her death completely unrelated to his mischievousness? Of course, as an adult he knew better, but as a kid, such thoughts aren't so absurd.

They were both quiet and still, and alone in their thoughts. The cuckoo clock clicked its rhythm. A soft, dependable rhythm. The air conditioner hummed its low ambient noise. Outside, an occasional meow or bark could be heard, while college-town traffic honked in the distance, all providing the soundtrack for Martin and Kathy's life that night.

And for a time, the bed made no noise.

Stuck in the Mud

The rain's early sprinkle had already created a post-dusty film on Clint Clay's old pickup truck's broad windshield. The mottled dust merely spread across the glass as the wipers slowly slid up and over and back down in an almost annoying repetition. Clint thought damn I wish I had refilled that wiper fluid. In the meantime, he simply had to wait for the sprinkle to work itself up into a harder rain, so that the window would finally clean itself, as he made his way along the dirt road that mere minutes ago had been hard and dry. Now, it was beginning to soften up. At first Clint welcomed the way the sprinkle held the dust down on the road; but, now as the remaining light of day retreated westward, it was hurried along by a deep purplish bank of storm clouds, prematurely darkening the sky and the view ahead. An occasional stab of lightning followed by an ever closer rumble signaled to Clint that his life was about to get messy, and quickly. He still had another sixty nine or so miles to go before he arrived at the large tin-roofed shed that served as a shelter and depot where he housed emergency stores and feed for his livestock, a few dozen head of Brangus cattle.

It had been a temperate fall this year, but that didn't

lessen his gratitude for the rain, the further relief from a previously record-breaking drought, and a further buffer from the devastating wildfires that had ravaged thousands of square miles of ranchland across the State. In those fires, Clint had lost 30 head, and he was forced to sell off an additional hundred head back East at a regrettable loss. Tonight, he was making sure the store of hay and feed he had amassed for the upcoming winter was protected. But now, for the last twenty-or-so miles, the rain had evolved into an insistent downpour, forcing Clint to slow down and pick his way through the ever-increasing slog. The bed of his pickup was heavy with supplies and a few covered bales of hay. The tarpaulin that he had tied down still held firm, he saw, and that relieved him.

It was while he was looking at his rearview mirror to check on the tarp that his truck slid off the road, jerking his steering wheel out of his hands for a second. He hit his brakes and came to a stop just off the shoulder and into a slight dip. It wasn't a ditch, and he checked to make sure he hadn't hit a railing or tree or fencepost. "Goddammit!" Clint said, hitting the steering wheel with both hands as if he was shoving away a bully at the bar. He righted the wheel as he pressed the accelerator pedal, but the truck only wiggled frustratingly and jarringly from side to side, barely inching forward in the rut he found himself in. "Shee-it," he whispered. "Shee-it, shee-it, shit."

He reached under the passenger seat and grabbed a heavy duty flashlight. He then fished a folded up rain poncho from his extended cab behind the seat. Muttering under his breath, he pulled the plastic over his denim jacket, put his cowboy hat back on and got out of the warmth and dryness of his truck. His boot sunk into the now water-filled crap-track his truck had just sloppily carved into the shoulder of the road.

He went 'round the back and saw what he had suspected: his right back tire was indeed stuck in the mud. And the rain continued to fall on him and on through the halogen beam of his Maglite. "It's gonna be a long night," he said, "because sooner or later some fool is gonna write a story about this inconsequential incident, and readers will wonder *What the hell was the point of THAT?*

And the author will shoot back: "Sometimes, the telling of a thing is better than the thing itself."

And isn't that exchange what makes almost all of life's inconsequential moments consequential, long after we get unstuck from the mud?

Ladybug

She's watching a concert on the lawn. A guitarist is singing songs by Townes Van Zandt. The guy next to her is attracted to her. She is really pretty, he thinks. She has auburn hair and red lips; she reminds him of Snow White somehow. She's wearing a polka dotted dress and flip flops. He wants her. He gets the feeling she likes him, too. Who knows? Maybe after the concert, they'll hook up.

Out of the corner of his eye, he notices a little ladybug crawling on a blade of grass by his chair. He watches it carefully as it makes its way up the blade and onto his pants leg. He's wearing jeans and the ladybug looks pretty against the denim blue. It is coming his way. It seems to know where it's going, but then just as it is about to crawl over the bend of his knee, the little beetle flies up and over to the auburn haired girl's knee. The ladybug looks so lovely, he thinks, as he watches the little wings pop open like the doors to that car from *Back to the Future* and flutter so effectively. It hovers but then moves toward the girl, with a force of purpose, it seems to him.

The ladybug alights on the auburn haired girl and begins to go this way and that, not quite knowing where to go. It stops and then resumes its crawl. By now, the auburn-haired girl has noticed the bug and she unhesitatingly flicks it off her leg, her knee now having become the end of a launching ramp. The ladybug is lost. He is saddened by this.

Later as he is fucking the auburn haired girl, the guy remembers the flicked ladybug. He wonders, just for a second, if he isn't just as bad as the auburn haired girl, because he knows it isn't going to be long before he brushes her off and never calls again.

The Haunted House

Before I died, I never thought I would live in a haunted house. I didn't even believe in ghosts. Now, I am one.

At the beginning, I wanted to stay around the house because it felt like home. I was free from the pain of the cancer, so I felt so good at first. I didn't really know what to make of it. I just knew I was free. Home, and free. I wandered from room to room. It took me a while to get used to the lack of physical limitations at first. Walking through doors wasn't my habit. It was strange. I would go for the door knob and try to twist it, but it wouldn't move. I finally realized, almost embarrassed by the simplicity of it, that I could just walk through doors. In fact, I stopped using doors altogether finally. I would just go through the wall.

I didn't have to stay, but I thought that was what I was supposed to do. I noticed that light everyone talks about, but I figured it could wait. I wasn't ready to leave. And my husband and son needed me, still.

So, those first few days were very sad. I saw them hurting. Saw them grieving about me. Saw them sob, together and alone. One night I went in to my son's bedroom just as he was waking up, and noticed that before his eyes opened, he wiped away a tear from his face. I had just tried to wick it away, but I couldn't remove his tears.

At first, my hanging around didn't feel awkward. It just felt normal. I would go about my regular routine. Watering the garden, sitting in my tv room where I would watch my soaps and read the newspaper. I would forget that I couldn't turn on the tv, but sooner or later, my son would come in and turn it on, and I would watch whatever show he tuned to. After a while, I tired of *Game of Thrones* and *Deadwood*. They were too violent for my tastes. I preferred the DIY shows and anything with Heidi Klum.

One day, right around the time they buried me, I couldn't help but notice the overwhelming grief my husband David was battling. He was despondent and I could sense he wanted to join me. What could I do?

In spite of my lack of physical pain, my beloved's mood made me ache in new ways. Of course, I wanted us to be together, but it wasn't time yet. And, I felt close to him, in a new way. After a lot of thought, I made an effort to communicate to him in the form of spontaneous thoughts I whispered to our son Charlie:

"Papa, you know what you've gotta do."

"What?"

"You need to go to the hardware store and buy a shovel."

"Buy a shovel? What are you talking about? I want to die. I just want to leave this world."

"I understand that, but there's so much work to do first. Before you die, you must buy a shovel and start

42

digging a hole. A hole of your own."

I was proud of Charlie, because now he took my train of thought as his, and carried it forward better than I could have imagined.

"A hole? Why would I want to dig a hole? All I want to do is leave this world and join my wife."

"I understand that, but there's too much to do. You must take care of her estate first, and buy her plot at the cemetery. And purchase her gravestone. All these things take tremendous effort when you're hurting so much, yourself. But, after each of these chores, you can reward yourself with a few shovel fulls of dirt for your own grave."

"No. It's too much. I just want to go to the river spillway and jump the rail and wash away."

"I understand that, too, Papa, but you mustn't do that yet. It would be wrong of you to leave without leaving a suitable hole."

"Every day, you must take care of these other matters. Call your lawyer; talk to the tombstone seller; write an epitaph; put the house on the market; give away her clothes; talk to the bank; settle the estate; and so on and so forth."

"And after each task, throughout the day, you must dig that hole."

"I see what you mean."

"Yes, you must go out and buy a shovel and dig your grave, Papa. You can't leave us until you have done so. Maybe by then, you won't want to leave us."

Over the next few months, I saw that David took care of business, lethargically at first, but a little at a time.

43

He called the tombstone man, the bank about my accounts, the lawyers about my will, and all the mundane things that still occur, as if nobody just turned the whole world upside down.

A year later, the night before the will was executed, I heard the following conversation between David and Charlie:

"Papa, you have done it. You have survived to see the estate matters nearly wrapped up. Tomorrow, we go to the lawyer's office to take care of mamma's will."

"Yes. It is finally here. I have somehow survived."

"It's a good thing you went out a bought a shovel!"

"Shovel?"

"Yeah—remember when I told you to go out a buy a shovel, so you could dig your grave?"

"I never bought a shovel!"

"I know you didn't. Not literally. But you still dug your hole day by day."

"I never dug a hole. I never bought a shovel."

"I know you didn't, Papa. I just meant, you couldn't leave this world yet, until you prepared your own estate and finished your business."

"I did it all. I never needed a shovel."

"I know. I'm not trying to take credit for your current wellbeing. I'm just saying, you were in a bad place, but your daily efforts kept you alive."

"My efforts. Not an imaginary shovel's."

"I know, Papa. You did it. But metaphorically you dug your hole. Now, whether you want to get into it is another matter."

"You never told me to buy a shovel."

"Why would I make that up? I was just giving you an image to envision. I know you didn't go out and buy a shovel and dig your grave."

"Damn right. I took care of business. I am a strong man."

"Exactly. You are a strong man. But you were a lot more vulnerable a year ago. And now you're better."

"I am better."

During the next few weeks, I noticed that my husband got back to his routine of keeping in touch with his friends on the computer. When I was alive, I hated that computer. It kept distance between us. He was always on it, and I always longed to have his full attention. I am not so sure that his obsession with that box didn't contribute to my stress and ultimately to my sickness. I hated that thing. But now, it kept him distracted from me. In that way, things hadn't changed much.

Later, I heard David and Charlie say to each other:

"I like how you said, buy a shovel."

"Oh, yeah? Well...that was a tough time."

Finally, I found that though I wanted to stay closer to my two loved ones, I just couldn't handle their habits. You can only accidentally walk in on your son pleasuring himself so many times before you just think, "It's time for me to go to the light."

Now, I am about to go. I would have stayed, but the living kept spooking me. They kept horrifying me with the actions they do in private. Some things are better left unknown.

The mysteries of death are difficult enough, but it's the things people do in the shadows that are much more troubling and scary. I didn't know that before, before I was a ghost. Now, I do. And it's high time I left my haunted house.

Poems

Migrant Birds

Swept by invisible brooms,
black birds, like words on a page,
specks of spilt ground
pepper blown in the wind,
much bigger though,
tightly—not randomly—
change course all
together, but not
altogether at the same,
exact moment.

So called "junk" birds
swim the skies, come north
for a while to make a life.
Ready now, they once again
become fluid spice, do their
instinctual dance, moved
not by whim, but fancy anyway,
and the hot pepper blows
home to southern climes,
seasoning skies elsewhere for a time.

Coffee House Sparrows

Now, they flit and flutter
From chair to chair, table to table, perch to perch.
The smaller one not far from the larger one, for very long
       anyway.

But, even house sparrows grow old and die someday.

Though some are killed by cats, or hit by cars, and others
       fly into glass that masquerades as clear, blue sky,
Do the others die of understandable exhaustion
From flying to and fro, finding their mates, preparing
       nests,
Getting food, and protecting their place,

Finally, just dying mid flight, heart bursting, causing that
Last plummet to ground—that last fall that His eye
       supposedly sees?

Or is it a slow and painful death, where sickness robs it
       of air
And ability to fly, period?

Or is it possible that one day they simply close their
       eyes and
Will their passage to the great beyond while they are
       asleep one last time?

Do their sparrow mates know that their sparrow mate
        has flown away forever?

Or do they awaken to silence, awaiting a first chirp of
        new day,
And not hearing it, know?

And having known a different heart failure,
Draw close to the other, smooth feathers, fold wings, and
        tuck head between breast and neck, and breathe,

Until, in silence, they die, too?

Go to the aftersky or an afternest
In an aftereave in the afterafter,
Where they aftersing, and afterfly,
And afterflit, and afterflutter,
And cause the afterlife also
To afterwonder
At their afterlove.

Lost Duck

Neck outstretched,
I strain to keep you
In my sights.

Lone duck, lost,
Circling high over
Head and homes.

Why alone?
In a summer sky
I can see it.

But in winter?
Where are your fellow
Anatini friends?

Neck outstretched,
You seem naked
Sans flanking hen and drakes.

Do you know
How lost you are?
Or did you choose, like me,

To dabble with solitude?

To My Stepmother, on Her Birthday

I keep scrolling through my photos,
Hoping a new one will appear.
One from yesterday, taken right
Before I went to work.
And I remember saying,
After the photo was snapped,
"Tomorrow, we'll have some
Fish for your birthday."
And as I left, you said,
"That will be nice."
And we hugged
And both said, "Tschüss."

But I only have this old one
Of you sitting next to the trail
Where we walked two years ago—
And another
Of your green-marbled tombstone
Placed over that space between memory
And wholeness.

Summer Lovers

He comes like a tourist who winds
his way from trap to trap, gawking,
buying things he can't live without,
carrying on as if each place was really
more than just a quickly fading memory
to be written down before it's lost.

He comes like a child who loudly
aches to ride a screaming carnival
ride, his face smeared candy-red
while wornout parents watch on, and
then moves on to the next amusement,
having forgotten the thrill of the last whirl.

He comes like a bee that bumbles
from flower to lurid flower, its legs
heavy with yellow powder that hitches
a ride to the next stop, then gets off
in a hurry to keep a date that she
couldn't possibly forget, but just might.

He comes like a man who kisses
her now, holding her head in his hands,
drawing her lips upward and close,
making her feel like she is his, only,
and then goes away as if he never
existed at all. Never. At all.

So, too, the writer comes, makes mark
on vellum or clay or paper or history,
on minds and hearts and souls, thoughts
made hard, words made flesh, then
leaves, and fades, and returns in the traces
that are read long after death, maybe.

Birds and Bees

Our lips make so little noise
When they come together,
But we do somehow produce
The mystery of song,
Of sound, of lyric and melody,
Like the ineffable vibrations
Of bumblebee wings, diaphanous
Shutters, holding up the body
That plunges into, back out of,
Finally alights on stamin and
Pistils, teasing its way inside
And tickling petaled depths
Until they come alive,
Like the purring of a cat,
Furry vibrator, inhaling,
Exhaling, whirring fluff-vibrations
Like those that come from
The friction of pen against paper,
The friction of two lovers
Fighting for the same space,
Like the fruit of words
Competing for life,
Words that wrap themselves around
The tiny bones in our ears,
Or the deep fissures in our minds,
Teasing us, teasing thought,
Until we are both spent.

My Ex-Wife

My ex-wife
Was an art teacher.
When she was in
A particularly
Good mood,
She would
Give me a
Paint Job.

"Elementary, My Dear"

Earth
Now, I wait under the mango tree,
looking into the shadows,
hoping that out of them
will come your light
to show me
what darkness looks like—
when it scatters.

Fire
My soul is a fire set ablaze
by accident (a bolt from
Heaven split my core,
turning to splinters
the stolid beams
of my certainties)
and your heat
has made my dulled heart
into slow-burning embers.

Air
So, hope sparks
upward like cinders
riding the fiery waves
into the sky.
Sprites fill the air
with magic dust

that will fall
back to earth
in the center
of life-giving raindrops.

Water
I asked the universe
for a drop;
it sent a monsoon instead.
That outpouring
washed away
everything
but my desire
for you.

Mourning Papers

*dedicated to Dr. Tom Pilkington, 1939—2011,
Professor of English, Tarleton State University,
and Ms. Marjorie "Jean" Foust, 1926—2011,
Tarleton State University's oldest graduating
English major, class of 1995, and my dearly
departed next-door neighbor*

Who ever knows
where the pages
to the books of our lives
will be found
or scattered?

Here and there,
some are folded
into our pockets,
some are tucked away
in manila folders
waiting to be read
at conferences or
in classrooms; others
are wadded up and
tossed aside, mistaken
for rubbish. Some are
first drafts of a chapter
that must be rewritten
over and over; others,

yellowed notes,
read and reread
for class, marked up
with the latest insights,
scratched out, underlined,
highlighted, with arrows
and circles and emendations
placed throughout
(only decipherable to you
and your closest readers).

Some are shelved
for later filing, or
donated to a library.
Others are misplaced,
temporarily or
forever. Some are
placed behind glass,
framed and put on walls.
Other pages are published
while we are alive
and able to celebrate,
and others are printed
only in a notice online
or in a newspaper
after our book appears
to be closed.
Some pages may be shredded,
but all are not disposed of
when the time comes.

Some are quoted from
in books yet to be
imagined, poems yet to be
written, and stories yet to be
read.

The Gentle Angler

He's been angling for years
(one way or the other)—rod,
reel, line, sinkers, bobbers,
and bait. He casts his line and
waits. The click of his reeling
becomes an uneven metronome,
keeping time, while he wastes
his, happily, with a hope
that is a pistachio bursting
green through its shell.

He goes again and again, slips into
the slow repetition, Jonquil
breezes, strong currents.
The Clementine sun shines
down; mind drifts cirrus slow,
remembering songbirds
collecting dappled dryer lint
for nests. And he takes nothing
home at all, and may never, as long
as he keeps fishing without a hook.

The Road to Topolobampo

The road to Topolobampo starts smooth and level,
A highway from Fort Worth, the Gateway to the
West, toward the mojo of Odessa/Permian and
The mountains at Fort Davis, where a man I once
Knew fell into a crevice on a hunting trip and died
There, wedged between two rocks. His shotgun
Did him no other good than to put himself out
Of his misery, which he did after about forty-eight
Hours, with an eerie crack still echoing, so they say.

We traveled south on the road to Topolobampo,
Past Alpine, and got out of our cars to see the Marfa
Lights, mysterious glows and halo-like teasers,
Thought to be car lights all the way from Mexico,
But that's unlikely, too, because it's probably just
Swamp Gas, swamp gas that takes on the shape of
UFO's and ghosts and urban legends and a reason
To stay at a hotel in Marfa, one of the most god-
Forsaken places you've ever seen. But I've seen worse.

We dropped off our car on the road to Topolobampo,
And took a cab to Ojinaga at the Texas/Mexico border,
Where we got on a bus that laced its way through
Northern Mexico to Chihuahua, a city as spread out
As a beautiful sombrero or a lovely dancer's dress.
We rented a car from there to begin our arduous drive
Into the Sierra Madre Occidental, a trip most people

Take by train on the Chihuahua al Pacifico Railway.
Ah, Chihuahua, what treasures were in store for us?

As we made our way along the road to Topolobampo,
We stopped in Cuauhtemoc for a Negro Modelo and
A Beefsteak. That was all the libation we dared to
Drink, for we would be driving into the Sierra Madre
The next morning, the Rocky Mountains of Mexico.
But first, that night, we would sit around a table,
Five men, forecasting our successes, as we dreamed
Of Topolobampo, the deepest port of Mexico's
Pacific Coast. The holy grail of the State of Sinaloa.

Next morning, we got back onto the road to
          Topolobampo,
Making our way to Divisadero where we perched
And looked out on the massive gorge, the Copper
          Canyon,
Which makes up part of the Sierra Tarahumara, covering
25,000 square miles, a system four times larger than
That canyon to the north, in the land of wealth, hype,
And unsurpassed public relations. While gazing upon
The gash deeper than the Grand Canyon, we felt ashamed
We had thought we were the only ones to have a canyon
          like this.

We met some mestizos on the road to Topolobampo,
The Tarahumara, masters of weaving, selling their
          baskets
For a few pesos each, but giving away their smiles

for free.
Colorfully dressed and impossibly diligent. Brown-
        skinned.
With orange and bright blue and red shawls. Fingers
        worn
Down but nimble and quick, making baskets—green at
        first,
But that turned different shades of light brown as
        they dried.
The Tarahumara wondered why we were driving our own
Car, not taking the train that brought them so many
        tourists.

On the road to Topolobampo, we stopped at Basaseachic
Falls, the fourth-highest cascadas in the Northern Hemi-
Sphere, the highest in Mexico. We walked underneath
To get a better look. We inhaled the mist, so gentle and
Ghostly, while the falls pounded into the pool,
        thundering
Its presence, shaking the land and the trees and the
        rocks.
This is also where we saw the roadrunner with the
        wriggling
Snake in its mouth, the brownish bird with the red visor
On its brow, stopping only long enough to subdue its
        prey.

Then, it was gone, and so were we, on the road to
Topolobampo. That night, we stopped again to rest and
Eat beefsteak with a quiver of fries and a slice of tomato

We were afraid to eat, having been warned not to eat
The vegetables unless they were certainly washed. We
Ate it anyway, on our way to Topolobampo, and none
Of us got sick. We slept hard that night in Yecora,
          dreaming
Of the flashing dolphins and glittering waters of the
Bay of Pelicans and Pongas and Shrimping Boats.

We wound our way on the road to Topolobampo.
Driving slowly through the Sierra Madre, I thought
To myself as I held onto the wheel: "Don't let us
Die. Don't let us die." I was praying to a God who
Had to know that Mexico was not the place I wanted
To die, though that would be so tragic and romantic.
The rockslide didn't hit our car, but it caused a
Traffic jam: a donkey, two trucks, a trio of cars,
And a dog that didn't seem to belong to anybody.

The road to Topolobampo eases its way out
Of the Sierra Madre into the Desert of Sonora,
Where all types of cactus and tumbleweeds are
Scattered against the backdrop of the sun-reddened
Foothills, where big black and brown specters move
Atop the highway, impossible, eight-legged creatures,
Crawling tarantulas, bigger than a man's outstretched
Hand, making their way across a road that they
Thought they had all to themselves, but didn't.

The road to Topolobampo makes its way along the
Coast down to Ciudad Obregon and then to Los

Mochis, where a Pennsylvanian farmer seeking
Fame and Fortune in the late 19th-century decided
To see how sweet his success might be with the
Sugarcane. While there, we asked a street vendor
About the last 30-mile stretch of road that would
Take us to our prize. His answer was quick and
Ominous: "El camino a Topolobampo es muy peligroso."

The road to Topolobampo is very dangerous,
The man on the street said, so we slept that night
In Los Mochis, where I saw a small owl the size
Of a Beanie Baby, looking out the mouth of a storm-
drain. It saw me, and scootched back, as if to say,
"I let you see me, but Mexico is not always so easy.
Sometimes, we are a bit more coy. Don't take me
For granted, gringo." I won't, I tell the owl. The
Next day, we will drive, forgoing bandidos tonight.

The last bit of road to Topolobampo is as smooth
As the first five-hundred miles out of Fort Worth.
When we arrived, the sea air touched our cheeks,
Patting us like a papá lovingly greeting his
Niños and niñas, after coming home from a long
Day on the shrimping boat. It felt good and
Familiar and familial at the same time. We rented
A ponga, a small boat, and chased the dolphins
And watched the pelicans dive bombing the sea.

The road to Topolobampo was the same road we
Took to get back home. Our adventures multiplied

As our car broke down in the mountains, under
A Mayan sky so full of stars that you could practically
Hear the satellites beep as they tracked across the
Canopy above our heads. We saw horses, locusts,
Eagles and cows; federales and checkpoints that
Sprang up out of nowhere, and towns with poverty
So deep, it put the Copper Canyon to shame, and us.

In Chihuahua, we dropped off our car, and ate burritos
With surprising chunks of pig rind, while waiting
At the bus station where two beautiful chicas asked
If they could come back to America with us. Their
Brown eyes and mocha-butter skin were hard to
Deny, but we had to say "no" on our way back
From Topolobampo. Later that night, we took
A taxi one last time from Ojinaga to Presidio, before
Heading back through West Texas on I-20 again,

The most deadly road of all, because it's so smooth
And so level and so sweet that its drivers can easily
Be lulled into sleep and oblivion. We made it home,
Though, tired but alive, the words of that vendor
Sounding in my ears, "El camino a Topolobampo
Es muy peligroso." And I thought, the road to
Topolobampo is very dangerous. But, in my mind,
All the roads we take, even the safe ones, are dangerous,
And in their way, they all lead to our own Topolobampo.

New Orleans: Three Haikus

Women bare their breasts
Freely, in exchange for cheap
Baubles, before Lent.

The City's music
Urges folks to practice for
Their above-ground graves.

Eat a beignet at
Café Dumond; Viet wait-
Staff count on your tips.

The Waist Land

(with apologies to T. S. Eliot)

Ignoscere me fascia sodes. (Forgive my girth, if
you please.)

Please, forgive my adipose fat,
especially the visceral, central fat.
You look at me now and wonder
how could I have ever wanted that?

We lie together, you and I,
or at least we used to
before my middle began to spread
like a lazy hooker, taking
her sweet time. Now, you wonder,
how could I have ever wanted
that? Please, forgive my adipose fat.

My hair is thinned, in arrears
to the scalp it once paid liberally,
and has been displaced to greater
frontiers, namely my shoulders,
back, and ears. Now I know you
wonder, how could I have ever wanted
that? Please, forgive my adipose fat.

At least the Buddha was seeking
a higher truth when he left behind

the frame of his youth. Now, he is
a forever one and I am just older,
writing these poems tucked into my folder.

Unfortunately, there is no paucity
of my central adiposity, and you'll
notice no great dearth of my
softly doughy midrange girth.

Please, forgive my adipose fat.
My visceral, central adiposity.
The fat in my belly that has
collected—and formed a barrier—
a cushion against the intimacy
we once knew when we coupled,
I on top of you, without pain
or gasping of breath. Without that
feeling of panic I have recently seen
in your eyes, though you have tried
to hide it. I don't mean to crush you,
don't want to make you look forward
to the relief of pressure that comes
from all that weight being lifted off
your lovely, petite frame. But, wait.
There's more.

Please, forgive my adipose fat,
my product of comfort food
and lack of motion. Don't call
it a beer belly, for you know I

don't drink enough beer for that
noble result. People respect you
if you drink beer, but not if you eat
Hostess® Cupcakes or SpaghettiOs®
with meatballs before sleeping.
And please don't call my adiposity
"love handles." I know better.
The love is waning as my belly waxes.
I don't need a spare tire and don't
want to chew the fat. I am waisting away
as it is. At least Buddha was cute,
and didn't want a girlfriend to bang
into. Please, forgive my adipose fat,
my visceral central adiposity. Help
me to curb my desire, my appetite,
my desire for more words that belie
my need for you. Help me to move,
move my body, move my pen. Please,
forgive my wasted words, for even my
adipose fat is a redundancy.

Let me start now with a paucity of letters.
Let me just say, please, forgive my fat,
for in spite of its effect on the distance
between your mouth and mine, your sex
and mine, my wanting and your lacking
I still, though you may find it hard to believe,
love you. I love you, me, and my adipose fat.

Dirty Sheets

I washed you out
of my sheets today.
No longer will the
smell of you haunt
my dreams.

Your skin that once
brushed against me
is gone now. Your
warmth but a phantom
that I sometimes think
I feel, but is really
no longer there.

Your breath naught
but a memory on my
neck, a ghost wandering
from pillow to pillow.

And so, I washed you
out of my sheets. But
not entirely. You still
linger in my pen, and
I can't exorcise you
from these sheets.

I can't wash you
away. For the more
I try, the more you stain
my clean, white sheets.

Nonfictions

The Time I Was Elvis

It was the summer of 1996, and I had just wrapped up quite a school year. The pressure to finish my doctorate was as high as it had been in a while. I had turned in the grades for my two classes I was teaching at the University of North Texas and my other two classes at Tarrant County College. Now, it was just "me" time, and I *had* to finish my dissertation. You see, I had already been hired as an assistant professor at a university in San Antonio and I needed to finish my Ph.D. work by August. So, there I was, sitting at my computer, working on putting into a thesis all that research I had done the previous three years, on Salman Rushdie.

The phone rang. It was my former roommate, Scott, whom I hadn't seen in over eight years. "Hey there, Moumin! How're you doin'? he asked.

"I'm doing great. Just working on my dissertation," I said.

"Well, I have a question for you. Would you marry me and my girlfriend in Las Vegas this summer? You are ordained, aren't you?"

Because I had gone to seminary before studying English at UNT, Scott just assumed I was an ordained minister. I wasn't. I had abandoned the idea of being a professional Christian quite some time ago. But I was intrigued.

"No, I'm not ordained. I just have a Master's in Biblical Studies. But, I'd love to marry you in Vegas. What's the deal?"

He explained that he wanted to get married in Las Vegas. Who doesn't? And that he wanted to be married by an "Elvis." Who doesn't? And that for his marriage ceremony to count when his Elvis officiated, his Elvis needed to be a legally ordained minister, too. This is where I came in.

"I'd love to!" I said, and bet him that I could get ordained on the relatively new thing called the internet. "Give me four minutes, and I'll get back to you."

Literally four minutes later, I called him back with a freshly printed up ordination certificate from the Universal Life Church, based in Modesto, California.

The Universal Life Church was originally set up as a protest against the tax exemption that is afforded to ministers. So, its founder gave out "ordinations" to anyone who would apply, so that they, too, could secure that same tax exempt status. I didn't care about the tax exemption, but I was happy that I could get the ever-important ordination authorization that would now allow me to do a wedding in Las Vegas, a town known for its weddings and very protective of their cottage (albeit a wedding cottage) industry.

So, while I was finishing up my dissertation, in the back of my mind loomed another deadline: July 3, the date that I was flying to Vegas with a fresh ordination and an

Elvis costume in my garment bag.

That was good. It forced me to aim for finishing my dissertation by July 3, so that my committee could look it over before my defense the following week, on July 9. What better distraction while your professors are evaluating your final draft than to take a working vacation to that oasis in the dessert, that playground in the sand, that haven of Elvis impersonators, and locus of the most spontaneous weddings in the U. S. of A.?

For a month and a half, I let my hair grow shaggy (yes, I actually had more of it back then) and my sideburns grow long. I picked up my outfit for the 70's Elvis—jumpsuit and scarf—and got all the arrangements set between Nevada (where I had to secure a license to perform a wedding in Las Vegas), California (where I had to secure the paperwork and signatures from the Universal Life Church on the Nevadan paperwork), and Texas (where I was getting my costume, finishing my dissertation chapters all at once, and letting my hair grow Elvis-ey).

I put together a very (surprisingly) traditional wedding script for Scott and his wife-to-be. They loved it. They wanted it to be serious, but just with an Elvis doing the officiating. (Okay. We all need different things to highlight our lives, right?) So, I incorporated all those elements into the wedding that I had seen all my life, growing up in Dallas, Texas. You know, "Do you take this woman to be your lawfully wedded wife? To have and to hold 'til death do you part?" All that. Thing is, I would be dressed in a garish white jumpsuit with gold trim, red scarf, and buggy sunglasses.

I couldn't believe that I did it, but I finished my other script, the one that would authorize my title of "doctor," and submitted it on the morning of the 3rd of July. That day, the wedding party was off to Las Vegas, for the wedding that would be held on July 4. Yes, I said it. July 4, 1999, in Vegas, as Elvis. And to top it off, it would be conducted at the Viva Las Vegas Wedding Chapel, between Freemont Street and the new Strip.

I had never been to Vegas before. What better way to start?

We stayed at Harrah's. I don't remember much about the day before the wedding other than I saw a lot of slot machines, ate a great buffet for little scratch, and walked the Strip just as the Bellagio and the Venetian were kicking off, and the new hotel casinos like Paris and New York, New York were still going up.

That night, I got ready for Scott's big day, and I couldn't have been happier to find a gold-covered Gideon Bible in my hotel room's night stand. It was perfect for the task I was about to fulfill the next day.

And I did.

As I walked through the lobby to the limo, Japanese (no, really) tourists stopped me to take a few pictures with an Elvis. I posed with my legs in that cocked frozen stride and my arms held in that mock stick-'em-up karate chop that He used to do back when He was alive in that very town.

When we got to the Chapel, the "real" Elvis impersonator was none too pleased that I was apparently horning in on his territory. I assured him that I was merely the minister and that *he* was the Elvis. He relaxed from that point on and did his part perfectly during the ceremony when I stepped aside after telling Scott and his new bride that they may kiss each other, to let him sing, "Love Me Tender."

The wedding was surreal. There I was, dressed as Elvis, at the Viva Las Vegas Wedding Chapel, standing there with a gold Bible (where else but Vegas would the "word of God" be packaged in a gold cover?), with a "real" fake Elvis behind me, while I did a rather traditional wedding for my former roomie.

When I got back to Denton, returned the costume, shaved my sideburns and got a haircut, successfully defended my dissertation, and began packing for my upcoming move to San Antonio, I couldn't help but wonder if perhaps my life couldn't get any better than that. Now, I had done what few people ever do: have their major professor call them "doctor" for the first time, and have strangers call out to them, "hey, it's Elvis!" all in the same week.

At the beginning of my career, I was Doctor Elvis, and then I started my real job. I've been Dr. Moumin Quazi ever since, but I must admit that every now and then, I crave a jelly donut or a peanut butter and banana sandwich late at night.

Thank you. Thank you very much.

What I Learned on My Summer Vacation, Ten Years Ago

On June 30, 2005, I accompanied a study-abroad tour with a group from the university where I worked, to Scotland, Wales, England, The Isle of Man, and Ireland. It was an exhilarating, grueling, and eye-opening trip, with a lot of time spent zipping from one place to another, with very little time to breathe. When I got home, to catch my breath, I wrote the following ten retroactive dispatches: "Things I Learned on the Trip."

July 4, 2005
I learned that the livestock in the Scottish, Welsh, and Irish countryside are luckier than the cows and horses here in West Texas. I never saw so many cows, sheep, and horses lolling in thick, green grass, lying around and taking their ease, as I did over there "across the Pond." And their good fortune made me wonder how any of us could ever take credit for being born somewhere like the U.S., when it's all just a kind of dumb luck-of-the-draw or by the hand of a mysterious God whose choices are to be wondered at, but never chalked up to our own merit.

July 5, 2005

I learned that frosted cereal can be touted on its box as "ludicrously tasty," and actually be telling the truth. We ate a variety of foods on the trip, including a variety of puddings, which don't resemble whatsoever "pudding" in America. Think bread pudding, rather than Jell-O brand pudding, and you're closer to what the Brits eat. Oh, and "blood pudding" is not as macabre as it sounds; it's actually a kind of sausage. Also, the fish and chips can be really good, battered just right and tender and flaky, or really junkfoody, just like certain foods here in the States. Also, I noticed that sometimes, the best food there was that which was brought to the British Isles from other places—for example, the curried dishes, the pizza, and of course, the most "British" thing in the world, tea (from India, by the way).

July 6, 2005

I learned that all these years, I've shortchanged the Romantic poets, especially William Wordsworth, whom I thought he wasn't as interested in Nature as he was in *writing* about Nature. When I saw Rydal Mount and Grasmere in the Lake District, where he lived and wrote, I thought much differently. That part of England is indescribably beautiful. When you look out the window of Wordsworth's study where he wrote, "poetry is the spontaneous overflow of […] emotion recollected in tranquility," I now understand that he didn't have to use his imagination that much to conjure the beauty of Lake Windermere or of the couple-of-hundred-year-old trees in his view, but that when he did write about daffodils or other aspects of Nature out of sight, he had some powerful memories to recall. Wordsworth wasn't one of those people who would say, hurry up and take the picture, so you can enjoy your present 2-minute visit later. Rather, I believe, he would say, luxuriate in the beauty now, live in it, drink in long drafts of life, and then you'll be fortunate enough, if you're a poet, to have something to later write about.

July 7, 2005
Our group always seemed to be on the fringe of—or in the wake of—huge events. For example, we arrived in Edinburgh, Scotland the day before the huge and peaceful "Make Poverty History" protest, which was coordinated with the Live 8 concerts held worldwide and the G8 Summit held just a few miles away at Gleneagles. I learned that not very many people in our bus of 29 folks could name the 8 rich nations represented there: the U.S., the U.K., Russia, Germany, Japan, Italy, France, and Canada. I learned that what makes the news there in Europe doesn't get much air time here in the States. For example, there were lots of protest riots in the nearby towns of Stirling and Bannockburn, the day after we left them. Also, the terrorist explosions on 7/7 (the Brit's nomenclature for their own 9/11) in London and that were eerily repeated on a smaller scale on 7/21, happened while our group was in Wales, visiting the town with the longest placename in the world:

llanfairpwllgwyngyllgogerychwyrndrobwllllantysiliogo gogoch which means, "Saint Mary's Church in the hollow of the white hazel near a rapid whirlpool and the Church of Saint Tysilio of the red cave." I learned that not being able to forget the song that helps you remember the pronunciation of that name may be the very thing that puts me in my grave.

July 8, 2005
I learned that the Jedi Library in Episode 2 of *Star Wars* was inspired by the Trinity College Old Library, a magnificent building that houses the *Book of Kells*, Ireland's most treasured artifact, besides the Guinness Brewery down the street. This dark-wooded, miles-of-shelves, two-story high library room housed the books that Jonathan Swift, Bram Stoker, J. M. Synge, Oscar Wilde, Samuel Beckett, Edmund Burke, and a slew of others checked out and found inspiration in. We remember the writers because they were great, but the legacy of Trinity College reminds us that they, too, were taught once.

July 10, 2005
I learned that when you travel on a bus together with a bunch of students and strangers, you can go on a 2-week trip without being formally introduced to not one, but two sets of parents or grandparents. And that's a shame, because I would have liked to have heard their stories. In the end, when you think about it, that's what we all have, whether we're American or European, peaceful or violent, Catholic or Protestant, Christian or Muslim, male or

female, Democratic or Republican, poor or wealthy, mobile or homebound, travelers or tourists—our stories. And those stories are what make this life, like the wheels on that un-air-conditioned bus we rode for the majority of our trip, go 'round and 'round.

July 11, 2005
I also learned that you have to watch what colors you wear in Ireland on certain days of the year. Just like you don't want to make the mistake of wearing red in the UT section at the Cotton Bowl, wearing orange is a bad idea in Ireland on July 12, the day that commemorates the Battle of the Boyne, the most famous Irish battle in its long history. The day is a sore point for the Catholic Irish majority, because it signals the imperialistic Protestant William III's victory over the Catholic James II at the River Boyne in 1690.

July 12, 2005
I learned that on a trip of any length, we're all annoying in our own way. Some folks may be late a time or two, others may whistle like a bird or make silly noises just to pass the time, others may talk incessantly, others may passive-aggressively ignore you, others may throw bits of paper at you when you're not looking, others may hold people to standards to which they themselves aren't willing to con-form, others may laugh too loudly, others may scowl too much, others may take everything personally, and others may unwittingly offend. If you go into a trip knowing that everyone, including yourself, will bother at least someone, somehow, then hopefully everyone will exercise a healthy

measure of grace and forgiveness with one another. At least it's a good thought.

July 13, 2005
I learned that Pat Boone still wears white shoes. He stayed at the same hotel that our group did in Ballybunion, Ireland, and I just happened to bump into him in the lobby. He was in Europe to sing at a concert. He's very gracious; he gave me an autograph that states, "To Moumin—God bless ya! Pat Boone." You never know when you're going to meet a superstar from another era, which brings me to my final entry.

July 14, 2005
I learned, as someone who traveled when I was a 21-year-old college grad I used to be versus the 42-year-old college professor I now am, that we, the teachers, the parents, the grandparents, the chaperones, really are an older generation; that the students who went on this trip really are our own inevitable replacements. They are now who we once were. And we will be whom they will grieve and remember. And they will be those who come to the realization one day that this world really is geared for the young who are here today and who are yet to be. And in the end, we will all, young or old, be forgotten someday, at least here on earth. But, I don't know about you, but I'm not ready, just yet, to be replaced. So, how about we all agree to live it up today! And hopefully, I'll see you on the next trip.

A Clean, Well-lighted Oven

Nobody told me how to be a man. I just picked up clues and hints along the way.

I learned that sometimes the best way to be a man is to fight the urge to be one. I'm talking about just plain old swallowing the first macho impulse, the pride, the ego that goes with being paternal and protective and, well, a man.

One of my models for manhood was my biological father, the man I call "Abba." He's from India and Pakistan, and once he visited me in Texas for a few months when I was in my early thirties. He was in the States from Germany where he had gone to retire with his German wife, Margo. His quadruple bypass heart surgery had gone well the previous year, but it was now time for his annual check-up, and he decided to stay with me for part of his yearly pilgrimage to the hospital in the States. His name was really "Man-zoor," and he was in his sixties, about five foot, nine inches, with a bald spot that had imperialized the rest of his crown, leaving only a few remnants of his formerly thick, black head of hair. The surgery had taken away his sturdy, robust build and replaced it with a bit of a frailty that I had never seen in him. He was still a solid man, though, with a strong will and an ever stronger capacity for expressing his controversial opinions. Remember those Munsingware shirts with the penguin logos? He wore them all the time. Casual. A pre-Izod, pre-Ralph Lauren Polo shirt. Abba's opinions seemed to pop up as surprisingly as those penguins that leap out of the antarctic waters and seem out of place stitched above a man's left-chest pocket. Abba's tranquil penguins hid the sense of dis-ease his shirts covered up. I remember the times he would berate the server lady behind the glass partition at Luby's for seemingly short-changing his portions: "Why are you giving me the short piece of broccoli?" like it was some pre-9/11 conspiracy to rob him of antioxidants.

I was living in a small, one-bedroom, one-bath apartment in the college town in north Texas I called home for about ten years while I was finishing my doctoral studies. When you're working on a Ph.D. in English, "studying" often looks like leisure. When people see that you are reading a book, they tend to think that you must be relaxing; after all, you're not really *doing* anything. Of course, we think differently about our "work." For this reason, students of literature tend to go off and work alone in a clean, well-lighted place—a room of their own, if you will. But this night, I decided to read at the dining room table while Abba was cooking.

The aroma of the spices hissed out from under the rocking pressure cooker weight, filling the room and apartment with a hint of Aurangabad and Karachi that my father had left over thirty five years before, when he immigrated to San Francisco to earn an MBA at Golden Gate College. All my childhood, I had heard terms like emm-bee-aay and

91

pee-atche-dee like they were words in and of themselves, not necessarily meaning Masters in Business Administration or Doctorate of Philosophy, but rather synonyms for high-paying positions in life. I think it disappointed my Abba that I was aspiring to be a professor instead of one of the hallowed five jobs he always mentioned when I was growing up—"one day, when you are an engineer, or a lawyer, or a doctor, or the president of the United States, or an astronaut, you will need to know how to use computers..."

The aromas of my Abba's cooking took me by surprise, reminding me of my childhood visits to Germany, where he was stationed as an internal auditor for the Army and Air Force Exchange Service. It was a tough job. Brutal on marriages. Requiring him to be gone for weeks at a time with only a weekend between auditing trips. When my mom told my Abba that she was filing for a divorce is the only time I ever saw him weep.

Like a magic carpet from *The Thousand and One Nights*, the pungency of the Indian blend of basmati rice, spices, and meats carried me away to a cave of sentimentality and remembrance. I was a child again, studying my schoolwork, and my abba was "Abba" again, cooking our meal like he used to after the divorce. As I continued to read my book, a part of my mind inventoried the spices whose presence made my bachelor-pad apartment feel like home. *Cumin, turmeric, bay leaves, cayenne pepper, and all-spice. The cloves that he put in the saffron-yellowed basmati rice.* Cloves. I hadn't thought about those little golf-ball-on-the-tee shaped stick of flavor in a long time.

Garlic, onions, sautéing in butter. Ginger. Fresh pine scent and bleach.

Fresh pine scent and bleach? I looked up quickly to find that Abba was filling a bucket with some hot water and toilet bowl cleaner. I didn't have any idea what he was doing.

"What are you doing?"

"I am going to mop the floor and clean the owen," he said with his Urdu-English accent. Owen was how he pronounced "oven."

"Oh."

Now, to be perfectly honest with you (a phrase that Abba was particularly fond of), I was annoyed by his sudden compulsion to clean the kitchen just minutes before our dinner was ready to eat. As far as I was concerned, the kitchen was free of roaches, so it was clean to me. But, if he wanted to clean the oven, spraying his brand new can of "Easy Off" into it, he was welcome to do so. When he came to stay with me, he said he would feel good about cooking and doing the dishes, and for me not to worry about such tasks. Rather he wanted me to spend my energy on my doctoral studies. Since he seemed to have a lot of time on his hands, being retired and far away from his home and wife in Germany, he didn't seem to mind cleaning up. Don't get me wrong. I cook, clean, and take care of myself when he's not there. It's just that it seems that when parents come to visit, old patterns of life reform and take shape again. That's what had happened with Abba and me.

Though I was grateful for the curried chicken with rice, when it was ready, I took my plate into my bedroom, mainly to get away from the fumes of cleaning solution. The meal was delicious, and I chuckled that as usual we weren't eating vegetables. Sometimes, it seemed like the healthy life was meant to be lived only when Abba's wife, my step-mother, was around. Margo, a vigorous and athletic German woman with blond hair the color of light sweet mustard, and cheeks colored not by blush but by actual, oxygenated blood, brought her rigor and discipline to everything she did. When she vacuumed, she combed the tassels of their Persian carpets with a pick; when we went on walks, they weren't leisurely, they were more like marches; when we ate meals, even the bread seemed to be more robust. Full of grains and heartiness. Margo would have made sure we had some vegetables with our meal, some broccoli perhaps, or some fresh carrots or snap peas, "Mit less rice, Mansuur," I can hear her saying.

When I was finished eating, I took my plate into the kitchen. Abba was already washing the dishes.

"I saved the owen for you," Abba said.

"Ohh-kaayy," I said back, with a little bit of an upward bend on the kay. The look on my face may have betrayed my seemingly innocuous response. I was starting to simmer towards a boil. He could tell that I wasn't very eager to interrupt my reading of Aldous Huxley's *Brave New World.* Before dinner I was getting to the description of the soma, a narcotic that helped people in the novel escape from their predetermined roles by taking a mental holiday. I was beginning to envy them.

By this time, Abba had situated himself like a baseball catcher in front of the oven, swabbing the insides clean with a big, yellow sponge. I guess he had given up on the idea that I might jump right in.

"Why have you never cleaned your owen?" he asked, his voice pinching out a higher tone when he said "never."

Batter up.

I thought for a second and began to formulate a response that admitted that I had no excuse, for I know that in life we choose to do only those things that are really important to us. The fact was, I didn't care about my oven. It didn't look dirty to me. I was naive, I suppose. And besides, what was he doing in my oven? The entire time he had visited, we hadn't made a single thing in the oven. It was all stove top cooking: a pressure cooker, a pot to make rice in, and that was it. What I managed to say was, "I don't have time."

"No, no, no." Strike one, two, and three. "The ting is, if you were to make cleaning the owen a priority, you vould take the time to clean it," he said.

"Abba, I totally agree with you, but what's up with your concern for my oven? Fifteen years ago, you would have been extremely comfortable in this apartment. In fact, it's a lot like the one you had when we visited you in Germany after the divorce. This place is no dirtier than that place was."

One of the mantras from *Brave New World* came to my mind. "Civilization is sterilization." Here my Abba was civilizing me, and sterilizing the life out of our time together.

But my abba was a man possessed. This is the same person who can't sleep for thinking about the squeaky door hinge on the other side of the house. Mind you, it's a hinge nobody is using. But he has to get up out of bed anyway, at 5:30 in the morning, waking the house, spraying WD-40 on all the hinges of every doorway and cabinet along the way to the squeaky one. "Possession" is the only word I know for that.

Apparently, he regrouped, and said, "I vant to tell you a story. I hope that it does not offend you."

* * *

You already know that any story that starts off with, "I hope this doesn't offend you," is bound to be really offensive. It didn't deter my Abba from bullishly proceeding.

"But I vant to tell you a story of someting that happened to me when I was about six or seven years old. Our family was living in India at the time. My abba and amma were away, and just my brothers and I were home. I remember an older friend of ours came over to the house and remarked how filty the house was, in spite of the fact that four strong, healthy boys were there. We had servants at the time, but it vas their day off. So, we hadn't bothered to clean the house. Anyvay, our friend asked the following question: 'How can you live in such filth? Don't you know that even a dog cleans the place it is about to lie on.'" Abba seemed to be happy with his rhetorical skills, for he just sat back and smiled.

"Even a dog knows better?" How do you respond to such an insinuation without taking it personally? People who know me know that I'm kind of a clean freak when it comes to my personal hygiene. You'll never catch me with dirty ears, that's for sure, but by my stepmother's

96

standards, and now apparently my Abba's, I was worse than a dog. In fact, I could hear Margo's voice in my head, too. "How could anyone with a set of healthy legs to work on and a set of hands to clean with live in such *schweinerei*, the obscenity of it all. Only a *schwein–hund* could live in such filth." A pig-dog. Somehow, in my stepmother's ontology, a person is essentially evil if he or she allows a dustball to collect in the corner of his or (*Ach du Lieber, Gott!*) her kitchen.

I thought it best that I walk into the other room to get my jacket and get out of the apartment for a bit, after all, I thought, "I don't live in my oven and I certainly don't sleep in it." But I understood his point. I said, "Abba, I'm surprised that this is all of sudden an issue. All those years when we'd come to visit you in your bachelor pad, you never once showed any signs of concern for your silly oven."

The silence that followed didn't change the tone of the ringing in my ears. What had started as such a fond memory had been clinically stripped of any warmth and nostalgia. He had cleaned a perfectly delicious meal of all its savor, and left it with the smell of Pine-Sol.

The man I loved so much when I was young, the man with whom my brother and I used to hang around late at night in our underwear watching super-8 movies of our childhood, who would ask if we wanted to go to Paris the next day, who would drive us out to Starnbergersee to walk past the spot where Mad King Ludwig, the king who built Neuschwanstein, the castle on the hill that inspired Disney's well-known icon, who would play Ravi Shankar music for us and cook basmati rice to go with our curried chicken

97

and keema—this man was hassling me about an oven? In a twisted way, he had gone native there in Germany, I guess.

But, as I was opening the door, he stopped swabbing the oven for a second, looked at me with the cutest expression I've ever seen on anyone's face, and said, with a blush that rose in his cheeks and flushed into his balding forehead, "You know, your uncle acted the same way last month when I confronted him about his filty owen, but I must tell you someting." Through a kind of giggle that I can only associate with shame, he said. "To be perfectly honest with you, in my entire life, I have only cleaned two owens, your uncle's and now yours."

And then he just smiled at me like a five year old who wants an ice cream cone, or a newlywed caught in his first lie, or an old man who knows he's full of shit sometimes, as he looked me in the eye, watching me smile back.